BENNY'S
BIRTHDAY PARTY

by Carol Kliszak

Copyright © 2020 Carol Kliszak
All rights reserved.

No part of this publication may be reproduced, stored in a retrieval system or transmitted in any way by any means, electronic, mechanical, photocopy, recording or otherwise without the prior permission of the author except as provided by USA copyright law.

Cover and Interior Illustration by Sarah E. Kurdziel
Published in the United States of America

Hardback ISBN: 978-0-578-60853-2
LCCN: 2020902389

JUV051000 JUVENILE FICTION / Imagination and Play
JUV054000 JUVENILE FICTION / Activity Books / General
JUV040000 JUVENILE FICTION / Toys, Dolls and Puppets

First Edition 2020
14 13 12 11 10 / 10 9 8 7 6 5 4 3 2 1

 # Dedication

I'm dedicating this book to all my grandchildren. The story line of this book was especially inspired by the youngest grandchildren, Rebecca Rappold, Sarah Kurdziel, and Stephen Kurdziel, who endeared these stuffed animals and held them close to their hearts.

Special thanks to my daughter, Kathy Miesowicz, for helping me put this book together and to my husband, Casey, for making it possible.

Everyone loves a birthday party, and Benny is no exception. He is a very loving monkey with little colored hearts all over him. About to turn five years old, he finds out he needs his friends to help him put his birthday party together.

Benny and his dear little friend, Oscar, a little brown lion, decided to put a birthday party together. Benny got the Happy Birthday streamers and Oscar got the balloons.

"SEE BENNY AND OSCAR WORK TOGETHER"

Oscar was too funny. He found out that if he held all the balloons at once, he would fly up, up, up in the air. Benny had to help him come down.

"SEE BENNY HELP OSCAR"

Oscar started hanging the streamers up, and got all tangled up in them. Benny helped Oscar by getting all the streamers off of him.

"SEE HOW FUNNY OSCAR LOOKS"

Benny and Oscar knew they couldn't do it all by themselves, so they had to call their friends for help.

"SEE BENNY AND OSCAR CALLING THEIR FRIENDS"

Lambie, a little pink lamb, said she would bake Benny's birthday cake. When she started, she got flour all over herself and on the walls and floor.

"SEE THE MESS LAMBIE MADE"

The La La Triplets, three little bears, were in charge of face painting, but instead got paint all over themselves and the floor.

"SEE THE FUNNY LA LA TRIPLETS"

Aiden, a cute furry puppy, was in charge of bringing the ice cream. He dropped some on the floor and it melted. Benny caught Aiden licking up the melted ice cream. Aiden got ice cream all over his ears and nose.

"SEE FUNNY AIDEN"

Lambie finished cleaning up the mess in the kitchen. She made the frosting and finished frosting Benny's birthday cake.

"SEE BENNY'S FUNNY BANANA BIRTHDAY CAKE"

The La La Triplets counted out five candles and put them on the cake.

"SEE HOW THE LA LA TRIPLETS CAN COUNT"

It was time to sing Happy Birthday to Benny.
All his friends gathered around him.

"SEE HOW HAPPY BENNY IS"

When Benny blew out his candles, he blew so hard that the candles flew out of the cake and up into the air.

"SEE FUNNY BENNY"

Everyone laughed and helped Benny pick up all the candles. Benny gave everyone a piece of cake.

"FUNNY OSCAR"

Benny looked at all the beautiful birthday cards his friends made for him. He will treasure them forever because he knew they were all made from their hearts.

"SEE THE LOVE BENNY GETS"

The La La Triplets wrote him a poem. Lambie drew a picture of her and Benny. Oscar said he would clean Benny's room for a week. Aiden said he would cheer Benny up whenever he was sad.

"SEE HOW FRIENDS STICK TOGETHER"

"THE END"

Draw a picture of Benny!

Draw a picture of your favorite stuffed toy!

About The Author: Carol Kliszak

I was born in Buffalo, New York. My interest in writing came at an early age. I wrote three songs that were recorded with a band. Making specialty birthday cakes for my family also gave me much enjoyment. Story time in our house was a learning experience filled with fun and love. I was inspired to write this book while watching my grandchildren show so much love while playing with their stuffed animals.

About the Illustrator: Sarah E. Kurdziel

This is the first book that Sarah E. Kurdziel has illustrated. She and her grandma, Carol, worked on the book together. Sarah is a junior in high school and is taking many art classes. Besides art, Sarah enjoys baton twirling at school football games, pep assemblies, and at the yearly school talent shows. She also enjoys spending time with family and friends. Sarah intends to pursue a career in the arts. Sarah's artwork can be seen on Instagram: sarahs__art_gallery.

Benny's Birthday Party

is a story about a little blue monkey and all his dear friends. He is a very loving monkey who is looking forward to turning five years old and wanting a fun birthday party. He finds out that he needs his friends to help him put the party together.

CPSIA information can be obtained
at www.ICGtesting.com
Printed in the USA
LVHW072013090320
649436LV00005B/527